HARMONIZATION OF FINANCIAL COOPERATIVE PRINCIPLES AND ISLAMIC FINANCIAL LAW FOR FINANCIAL INCLUSION

GETACHEW MERGIA TACHE

AUGUST 2024, SEATTLE, USA

HTTPS://BRIGHTFORCOOPERATIVES.ORG/

CONTENTS

Acknowledgment

I extend my heartfelt gratitude and special appreciation to the dedicated trainees in Cooperative Business Promotion and Management in Ethiopia. These individuals were thoughtfully chosen from diverse regions of Ethiopia, including Somali, Afar, and Benishangul Guemuze regions, to participate in a Training of Trainers (ToT) program for Rural Financial Cooperative/Rural SACCOs organized by the Ethiopian Federal Cooperative Commission Rural Financial Intermediation Programme (RUFIP) Coordination Unit. This ToT training program took place from December 15 to 29, 2004 at Pan-Afric Hotel, Adama City, Oromia Region, Ethiopia, during which I had the privilege of serving as a Senior Trainer. The primary objective of this training was to enhance the expansion of Rural SACCOs in Muslim-dominated regions. Throughout the Rural Financial Cooperative/Rural SACCOs Promotion & Management ToT training, the participating trainees presented insightful questions that challenged me to explore ways of aligning traditional financial service practices of SACCOs with Islamic financial principles. Their inquiries were pivotal, particularly in addressing the unique needs and beliefs of broader rural Muslim populations and contributing to the growth of Rural SACCOs in those regions. In response to this challenge, I threw back the ball to the trainees by facilitating a three-day group discussion workout session to make them come up with a local solution, empowering the trainees to collaboratively devise a practical and acceptable strategy resonating with the broader target rural Muslim populations.

This three-day group discussion workout session also provided me with the time and opportunity to read more and deepen my understanding of Islamic financial principles and practices, better equipping me to guide the training using a participatory approach. With the majority of trainees being Muslim, they formulated a strategy in those group discussion workout sessions that harmonized well with the beliefs of the broader rural Muslim population regarding the utilization of financial services. Finally, together we redefined the training, making it more productive, and generated the initial draft direction on how to promote and manage Rural SACCOs in those Muslim-dominated regions. This experience acted as a catalyst for my further exploration of ways to align Financial Cooperatives' principles with the Islamic Financial System. I express my sincere appreciation for the invaluable input provided by the trainees, who inspired me with the idea of finding a way of harmonizing the financial cooperatives and Islamic Financial practices; with the ultimate goal of deepening and ensuring financial inclusion for the majority facing exclusion in today's financial market system. As a result, after I studied Islamic financial principles and practices for many years, I am motivated to write this guidebook on the **"Harmonization of Financial Cooperative Principles and Islamic Financial Law for Financial Inclusion,"** In response to that challenge.

A special acknowledgment is extended to the professionals who supported and encouraged me to make this modest contribution to the financial inclusion of excluded **Muslim Populations Globally**.

The Author

Getachew Mergia Tache, a specialist in financial inclusion and Cooperative-based community economic development. Holding a spectrum of professional certifications, including Market System Development (M4P), Rural Finance, Value Chain Finance, Agricultural Goods Lease Financing, SME Finance, and Microfinance, he stands as a recognized expert. The Ethiopian Management Institute has qualified him professionally as a consultant specializing in Cooperatives, Financial Cooperatives, and Community-based Economic Development.

Getachew's expertise is a result of comprehensive training in promoting and managing cooperative enterprises and community-based economic development, courtesy of Mekelle University and Makerere University. Armed with a BSc in Agriculture (1994) and an MA Degree in Cooperative Marketing (2010), he boasts over 25 years of rich experience that spans both the private and public sectors.

Notably, Getachew underwent on-the-job training as a Rural SACCO promotion and management expert facilitated by ACDI/VOCA from Jan 1, 2001, to Dec 31, 2003. Additionally, he successfully completed a certified Microfinance Expert program facilitated by the Frankfurt School of Finance and Management. His commitment to continuous learning led him to the Market System Development-Making Market Work for the Poor (M4P) Training held at the Springfield Development Centre in Bangkok, Thailand.

With a wealth of experience, Getachew has played diverse roles in Financial Inclusion, Rural Finance, SME Finance, Agricultural Value Chain Finance, and Cooperative Development. His contributions have left an indelible mark in both Ethiopia and Uganda.

I. Abstract

- ## Importance of the Book:

In the Introduction, the book sets the stage by highlighting the significance of harmonizing financial cooperative principles with Islamic financial law for achieving financial inclusion. It contextualizes the growing importance of Islamic finance globally, especially in regions with sizable Muslim populations like Africa. By addressing the needs of this demographic, the book establishes its relevance in addressing a pertinent issue in today's financial landscape. The credibility of the book is established by outlining the challenges faced by underserved Muslim communities, providing a clear context for the necessity of its intervention. This book becomes useful as it offers a comprehensive guide for financial cooperatives, policymakers, and stakeholders interested in fostering financial inclusion through the integration of financial cooperative principles with Islamic financial law.

- ## Challenges and Obstacles Addressed:

The book identifies several challenges hindering the harmonization of financial cooperative principles with Islamic financial law. These challenges include the lack of awareness among stakeholders, legal and regulatory hurdles, capacity-building issues, and resource allocation constraints. Failure to address these challenges could result in continued financial exclusion for Muslim communities, exacerbating socioeconomic disparities and limiting economic growth potential. The book's intervention is necessary to bridge these gaps and pave the way for inclusive financial practices that align with Islamic principles, ensuring equitable access to financial services for all.

- **Unique Solution and Approach:**

This book proposes a unique solution by offering a comprehensive framework for integrating Islamic finance principles into the operations of financial cooperatives. It outlines specific strategies such as educational awareness programs, collaboration with policymakers and regulatory bodies, capacity-building initiatives, and resource allocation planning. What sets this intervention apart is its holistic approach, addressing challenges at multiple levels and providing actionable solutions tailored to the needs of financial cooperatives serving Muslim communities. By focusing on the harmonization of financial cooperative principles with Islamic financial law, this book ensures a culturally and ethically resonant approach to financial inclusion, distinguishing it from other interventions that may overlook these nuances.

- **Expected Advantages and Results:**

The intervention outlined in this book promises numerous advantages and results for stakeholders and the broader targeted community. Financial cooperatives stand to benefit from enhanced operational capabilities, improved regulatory compliance, and increased market relevance. Members of underserved Muslim communities gain access to Shariah-compliant financial services tailored to their specific beliefs and needs, fostering economic empowerment and social inclusion. Additionally, policymakers and regulatory bodies benefit from a more inclusive financial ecosystem, contributing to broader inclusive economic development goals. Indirectly, the entire community benefits from a more equitable distribution of financial resources, leading to greater stability and inclusive, equitable economic development. Overall, the intervention outlined in this book holds the potential to transform the financial landscape, creating opportunities for all stakeholders and driving sustainable growth and broad-based development.

• **Vast Untapped Market of Muslim Communities**

The importance of this book for financial cooperatives aiming to benefit from the vast untapped market of Muslim communities globally is highlighted by the significant access to finance gap within this demographic. Despite certain countries initiating efforts to endorse and promote Islamic finance products, a substantial deficit in infrastructure development persists. This deficit poses a challenge to enhancing financial inclusion and effectively serving the currently excluded and potentially expanding Muslim populations.

This book is crucial as it offers a strategic roadmap for financial cooperatives to navigate and bridge this gap. By advocating for the harmonization of financial cooperative principles with Islamic financial law, the book provides a comprehensive framework tailored to the needs of these communities. This approach not only acknowledges and respects the unique cultural and religious considerations of Muslim populations but also presents financial cooperatives with an opportunity to tap into a sizable and growing market segment.

Moreover, the intervention advocated in this book addresses critical challenges such as awareness gaps, regulatory hurdles, and capacity limitations that currently hinder inclusive financial practices. Through targeted education, collaboration with policymakers, and strategic resource allocation, financial cooperatives can enhance their operational capabilities and regulatory compliance. This, in turn, facilitates economic empowerment and social inclusion within Muslim communities.

The holistic approach outlined in this book promises tangible benefits for financial cooperatives and policymakers alike. Financial cooperatives stand to gain increased market relevance and operational efficiency, while policymakers benefit from a more inclusive financial ecosystem that aligns with broader economic development goals. Ultimately, members of underserved Muslim communities benefit from access to ethical and culturally sensitive financial services, paving the way for more equitable economic development and social progress.

In summary, this book serves as a vital tool for financial cooperatives seeking to tap into the significant market potential presented by Muslim communities globally. By addressing infrastructure deficits and advocating for the integration of Islamic finance principles, the intervention outlined in this book not only addresses critical challenges but also fosters sustainable growth and inclusive economic development within these communities.

II. Introduction

Background

Numerous studies have unequivocally shown that in countries with low financial inclusion, there is a direct correlation to persistent income inequality, sluggish economic growth, and heightened instability, as it excludes the majority from reaping economic benefits. Low financial inclusion excludes most people from enjoying the advantages and positive outcomes that come with participating in and benefiting from economic opportunities. IMF data indicates there is a significant worldwide gap in access to finance. Improving financial inclusion, therefore, not only bridges this gap but also creates economic opportunities for the excluded majorities, fostering resilience, growth, and stability in countries.

This paper will focus on exploring ways to possibly enhance financial inclusion among those who have voluntarily excluded themselves from using existing financial services due to religious and cultural reasons in Africa, thereby coming up with a strategy for enhancing financial inclusion, particularly to motivate those who have voluntarily chosen to abstain from using existing financial services for cultural and religious reasons. As a strategic intervention, this paper involves investigating the potential area of Harmonization between Financial Cooperative Principles and Islamic Financial Law for achieving greater financial inclusion among those voluntarily excluded populations.

The existing financial landscape often misaligned with Islamic religious beliefs and lacking Shariah-compliant products, has widened the financial inclusion gap among Muslim communities. The discrepancy between these facilities and religious principles has led many to abstain from utilizing available financial services. Addressing this, an exploration of Islamic finance practices[1] becomes imperative to bridge the gap in financial inclusion.

The investigation into the synergy between these two financial practices is driven by the urgency to determine potential conflicts or alignments. Understanding how cooperative principles and Islamic financial law can harmonize is crucial for advancing financial inclusion. Financial inclusion, ensuring access to affordable and pertinent financial products and services, is a vital enabler for poverty reduction and overall prosperity by engaging the excluded majority in the market.

Financial cooperatives/ SACCO Societies form the cornerstone of an organizational philosophy rooted in self-help, self-reliance, mutual assistance, democracy, and solidarity. Guided by ethical values like honesty, openness, social responsibility, and care for others, these cooperatives prioritize human needs over profit maximization. They were established to counter exploitation, rectify market distortions, and foster genuine market competition.

Islamic financial law seamlessly aligns with cooperative values, emphasizing brotherhood and solidarity while prohibiting interest to prevent exploitation. Shared principles of profit and loss echo Financial cooperatives/SACCO 'Societies' "Member Economic Participation" principle. Islamic financial instruments prioritize equity, with Islamic banks operating as partners, sharing risks and gains collaboratively. Solidarity is evident in financial products designed without remuneration, and Islamic institutions allocate funds from surplus for social purposes, aligning with the "Concern for Community" principle of Financial cooperatives/SACCO Societies.

In conclusion, a genuine application of cooperative principles and Islamic financial law reveals a harmonious coexistence without inherent conflicts. Financial cooperatives/SACCO Societies possess

---

1. Islamic finance refers to how businesses and individuals raise capital in accordance with Shariah-compliant

the potential to efficiently provide compatible financial services to low and middle-income Muslim communities, supporting the real economic sector and promoting societal well-being through share-based financing.

Keywords: Financial Cooperatives, SACCO Societies (Credit Unions), Cooperative Principles Islamic Financial Law, Islamic Financial Institutions, Financial Inclusion, Muslim populations.

Financial Inclusion Gap in countries with significant Muslim populations

Africa[2] has the largest percentage of Muslim population, approximately 52.29%, with 33 African countries having a Muslim population ranging from 20% in Mozambique to 100% in Somalia[3]. The Muslim population in Africa is projected to grow by nearly 60% in 2030[4]. However, there exists a substantial access to finance gap within the Muslim population in Africa. Despite some African countries taking steps to support and promote the development of Islamic finance products, a significant infrastructure development deficit requires improvement to enhance the level of financial inclusion and serve the currently excluded and potentially growing target populations. Some traditional banks across the continent have also begun offering Shari'ah-compliant banking products through "Islamic windows." The data from randomly selected Muslim population-dominated African countries indicates that the exclusion level ranges approximately from 30 to 56%. For example **Morocco** approximately only 44% have access to financial services, leaving 26.2 million Moroccans without access to a bank

---

2. The continent has a Muslim population of approximately 742 million, Muslim Population in Africa
3. Muslim Population in Africa
4. The Future of the Global Muslim Population. Today Globally there is 29.90% of Muslim Population, Asia has 33.32%, EU 7.63%, North America 1.08% and South America 0.41%, and Oceania 1.85%.

account[5]. In **Tunisia,** around 30% to 40% of the adult population and more than half the enterprises remain unserved or underserved by the mainstream financial sector[6]. In **Nigeria**, More than 28.8 million Nigerian adults are still excluded from accessing financial services, no access to useful, relevant, and affordable formal financial services[7].

The Financial Inclusion Gap in African countries demands the engagement of alternative financial institutions like financial cooperatives by creating enabling policies to harmonize the application of financial cooperative principles and Islamic financial law.

Numerous studies have shown low financial inclusion excludes most people from enjoying the advantages and positive outcomes that come with participating in and benefiting from economic opportunities. IMF data indicates there is a significant worldwide gap in access to finance. Improving financial inclusion, therefore, not only bridges this gap but also creates economic opportunities for the excluded majorities, fostering resilience, growth, and stability in countries.

However, to improve and increase financial inclusion, understanding the key factors of exclusion is crucial. Studies indicate two types of financial exclusion: involuntary and voluntary. Involuntary exclusion arises from factors such as insufficient income, high-risk profiles, discrimination, and market failures. In contrast, voluntary exclusion occurs when individuals or firms choose not to use financial services due to cultural, religious, or other reasons.

This paper focuses on exploring ways to enhance financial inclusion among those who have voluntarily excluded themselves from existing financial services due to religious and cultural reasons in Africa. The goal is to devise a strategy that motivates individuals who have volun-

---

5. Financial Inclusion in Morocco, IMF Morocco's National Strategy for Financial Inclusion by Lorraine Ocampos,
6. Financial Inclusion in Tunisia : Low-Income Households and Micro-Enterprises, WorldBank publication
7. https://www.cbn.gov.ng/DFD/Financialinclusion.asp

chosen to abstain from using existing financial services for cultural and religious reasons. As a strategic intervention, this paper investigates the potential area of Harmonization between Financial Cooperative Principles and Islamic Financial Law to achieve greater financial inclusion among those voluntarily excluded populations, considering the significant financial exclusion level within Muslim populations in Africa.

In conclusion, the pervasive Financial Inclusion Gap in African countries calls for immediate attention and innovative solutions. The engagement of alternative financial institutions emerges as a pivotal strategy to address this challenge. Specifically, financial cooperatives present a promising avenue for fostering inclusivity. The key lies in harmonizing the application of financial cooperative principles and Islamic financial law. This Harmonization offers a unique opportunity to create a financial cooperative ecosystem that is not only inclusive but also aligned with ethical values. Leveraging the principles of financial cooperatives, rooted in self-help, mutual assistance, and democratic values, and integrating them with the ethical underpinnings of Islamic financial law, can facilitate the way for more equitable and accessible financial inclusion-based services for the excluded broad Muslim community.

This strategic intervention holds immense potential to cater to the needs of those voluntarily excluded from mainstream financial services due to religious and cultural reasons. As we navigate the challenges presented by the significant financial exclusion levels within Muslim populations in Africa, this approach can act as a catalyst for change.

In essence, the call to action is clear: to bridge the Financial Inclusion Gap in African countries, we must embrace alternative financial institutions and facilitate a seamless integration of financial cooperative principles and Islamic financial law. This not only represents a pathway to financial inclusion but also embodies a commitment to building a more just, resilient, and prosperous economic future for all.

Existing financial facilities and Islamic religious

In many African countries the existing financial facilities, primarily designed for traditional financial services, stand in contrast to Islamic Shari'ah-compliant financial mechanisms. This contradiction significantly contributed to the financial exclusion among Muslim communities. These factors prompt many individuals to avoid utilizing existing financial facilities. Consequently, millions are left without access to finance, necessitating a critical exploration of Islamic finance law practices that could potentially harmonize with financial cooperative principles and practices to address this impediment to the financial inclusion of Muslim communities in Africa.

The investigation into the relationship between cooperative principles and Islamic financial law is motivated by the need to determine potential conflicts or synergies. Understanding the possible alignments between cooperative principles and Islamic financial law is crucial for fostering Financial Inclusion among the voluntarily excluded Muslim communities in Africa. Financial inclusion, defined as ensuring individuals and businesses have access to affordable and useful financial products and services, encompasses transactions, payments, savings, credit, and insurance—all delivered in a responsible and sustainable manner. This inclusive approach is considered a pivotal enabler for poverty reduction and the enhancement of prosperity[8]. The issue at hand is how the widened financial inclusion gap among Muslim communities can be narrowed to an acceptable level. If the existing traditional financial services in most African countries stand in contrast to Islamic Shari'ah-compliant financial mechanisms, can financial cooperative practices possibly align with Islamic financial law?

Financial cooperatives serve as the bedrock of an organizational philos-

---

8.   World Bank, https://www.worldbank.org/en/topic/financialinclusion/overview

grounded in emphasizing self-help, self-reliance, mutual help, democracy, and solidarity. According to ICA[9].

On the other hand, Islamic financial law aligns with cooperative values, emphasizing brotherhood and solidarity. It prohibits interest to prevent exploitation, aligning with cooperative motives. Both systems share principles of profit and loss sharing, similar to the "Member Economic Participation" principle of financial cooperatives/SACCO Societies. Islamic financial instruments prioritize equity, and Islamic Financial institutions operate with clients as partners, sharing risks and gains. Solidarity is a fundamental principle in both systems, evident in financial products without remuneration. Islamic financial institutions may retain funds from surplus for social purposes, aligning with the "Concern for Community" principle of SACCO Societies.

In conclusion, there is no conflict between Islamic financial law and cooperative principles, a genuine application of cooperative principles and Islamic financial law reveals a harmonious coexistence without inherent conflicts. Financial cooperatives/SACCO Societies, therefore, have the potential to provide Shari'ah-compliant compatible financial services efficiently and competitively to low and middle-income Muslim communities. Hence, supporting Financial cooperatives/SACCO Societies' engagement through shariah-based financing can support the real economic sector, promoting overall societal well-being for society as a whole.

Rationale: Exploring Cooperative Principles through the lens of Islamic Finance

The exploration of cooperative principles in the context of harmonizing with Islamic finance for the strategic financial inclusion of Muslim communities is driven by several compelling reasons :

---

9. The International Cooperative Alliance (ICA) is a non-governmental cooperative organization founded in 1895 to unite, represent and serve cooperatives worldwide.

• Alignment of Values: Cooperative principles and Islamic finance share foundational values such as solidarity, equality, and social responsibility. Exploring their alignment can reveal synergies that contribute to ethical and socially responsible financial practices in serving the excluded Muslim communities in Africa.

• Philosophical Harmony: Both cooperative principles and Islamic finance aim to create a socio-economic order based on fairness, justice, and mutual support. Examining their philosophical harmony can enhance understanding and foster collaboration between the two systems in order to serv the excluded Muslim communities in Africa.

• Ethical and Social Impact: Cooperative principles emphasize ethical values and social impact. Islamic finance, rooted in brother-hood and social order, has similar objectives. Investigating the potential integration of cooperative principles can enhance the ethical and social impact of Islamic financial practices to boost financial services among the excluded Muslim communities in Africa.

• Financial Inclusion: Cooperative principles, particularly those of Financial cooperatives/SACCO Societies, focus on financial inclusion and empowering low-income individuals. Evaluating how these principles can complement Islamic finance may lead to inclusive financial solutions for Muslim communities, especially in less developed countries (LDCs).

• Risk and Profit Sharing: Both systems prioritize risk and profit sharing among members. Analyzing the cooperative principles within Islamic finance can provide insights into creating financial instruments that align with the cooperative model, fostering a sense of shared responsibility.

• Enhancing Community Well-being: Cooperative principles and Islamic finance share a commitment to community welfare. Exploring cooperative principles within Islamic finance may lead to innovative approaches that contribute to the well-being of communities, aligning with the values of both systems.

• Global Financial Inclusion Initiatives: Given the global emphasis on financial inclusion and sustainable practices, exploring the integration of cooperative principles in Islamic finance can contribute to international initiatives promoting responsible and inclusive financial systems.

• Operational Guidelines: Cooperative principles provide operational guidelines for cooperatives. Evaluating their applicability within Islamic finance can offer practical insights into structuring financial institutions that prioritize member needs and community development.

In summary, exploring cooperative principles in Islamic finance is driven by the desire to enhance ethical, inclusive, and community-focused financial practices through Financial Cooperative. The rationale lies in uncovering potential synergies that can lead to the development of financial systems that prioritize the well-being of individuals and communities in accordance with cooperative and Islamic principles to contribute to Global Financial Inclusion Goals[10].

---

10. Mar 29, 2022 — The World Bank Group considers financial inclusion a key enabler ***to reduce extreme poverty and boost shared prosperity.***

III. Understanding Cooperative Principles

A. Definition and Overview of Cooperative Principles

A cooperative is a type of organization or business that is owned and operated by its members for their mutual benefit. It is guided by a set of principles that distinguish it from other forms of business entities. Cooperative principles provide a framework for democratic and member-driven decision-making, emphasizing the well-being of the community. According to the International Cooperative Alliance (ICA), key aspects of cooperative principles include:

1. Voluntary and Open Membership: Cooperatives are open to all individuals who are willing to accept the responsibilities of membership without discrimination.

2. DemocraticMember Control: Members have an equal say in the decision-making processes, and decisions are made democratically, typically following a "one member, one vote" system.

3. MemberEconomic Participation: Members contribute equitably to the capital of the cooperative. The economic benefits derived from the cooperative's operations are distributed among the members based on their transactions with the cooperative.

4. Autonomy and Independence: Cooperatives are autonomous, self-help organizations controlled by their members. They make decisions independently, keeping in mind the best interests of the members.

5. Education, Training, and Information. Cooperatives provide education and continuous training to their members, leaders, and their community, empowering them to contribute effectively to the development of the cooperative and to make the best use of resources for themselves and the community.

6. Cooperation among Cooperatives: Cooperatives work together for their mutual benefit by forming alliances and collaborating

with other cooperatives. This alliance of collaboration among cooperatives could be at the local, regional, national, or international level.

7. Concern for Community: Cooperatives strive for the sustainable development of their communities. They contribute to the well-being of the community by addressing local needs and promoting social responsibility.

B. Core Values of Cooperatives

The core values underpinning cooperative principles include:

1. Self-Help: Members take initiative and responsibility for their economic well-being.

2. Self-Responsibility: Members actively participate in the decision-making process and take responsibility for the success of the cooperative's planned activities.

3. Self-Financing: Members, as owner-user-investors, take initiative and responsibility for the success of the cooperative through continuous members' share capital and business patronage based on internal capital formation.

4. Democracy: Democratic decision-making ensures equality and fairness among members as well as enhances a sense of ownership among members.

5. Equality: All members have equal rights and opportunities within the cooperative.

6. Equity: Benefits are distributed fairly, reflecting members' capital contributions and patronage transactions.

7. Solidarity: Members work together for mutual benefit, fostering a sense of community and shared purpose.

8. Honesty and Openness: Transparency and open communication are vital for trust and integrity within the cooperative.

9. Social Responsibility: Cooperatives prioritize social and environmental considerations in their operations.

C. Cooperative Principles in International Context

Cooperative principles have global applicability and are recognized internationally. The International Cooperative Alliance (ICA) is a global association that establishes and promotes these principles. While variations exist, the core principles are widely accepted and applied across diverse cooperative sectors worldwide. These principles, initially set by the Rochdale Cooperative in England in 1844, form the foundation of the core cooperative principles and values. While there may be some variations, the core principles are widely embraced across different cooperative sectors worldwide. The ICA emphasizes the importance of these principles for fostering sustainable development, economic resilience, and community well-being on a global scale. The principles are adaptable to various cultural and economic contexts, providing a universal framework for cooperative enterprises.

IV. Understanding Islamic Financial Law

A. Basic Principles of Islamic Finance and Key Compliance and Instruments

In the realm of global finance, the interplay between financial cooperative values and the principle of Islamic finance stands as a promising avenue for driving financial inclusion and fostering ethical community-based economic development. This synergy is built upon the foundational tenets of Islamic finance, which encompass the prohibition of interest, avoidance of speculative practices, and strict adherence to Shariah law. As we embark on an exploration of this harmonious relationship, it is imperative to understand the basic principles of Islamic finance, investigate the distinctions of Shariah compliance, and gain insights into the diverse array of Islamic financial instruments. By aligning these principles with financial cooperative values, we aspire to unlock the potential for financial inclusion and contribute to a sustainable and inclusive economic landscape.

1. Basic Principles of Islamic Finance:[1]

- Prohibition of Interest (Riba): Islamic finance strictly prohibits the payment or receipt of interest, as outlined in the Quran.
- Avoidance of contractual uncertainty and gambling (Gharar and Maisir): Islamic finance condemns contractual uncertainty (gharar) and gambling (maisir) in financial transactions.
- Avoidance of Haram Industries: Transactions involving prohibited industries such as pork products, pornography, or alcoholic beverages are strictly forbidden in Islamic finance.
- Compliance with Shariah: All financial activities must adhere to the principles established by Shariah law, guided by rulings (fatwa) issued by qualified Muslim scholars. etc.

---

1. https://aaoifi.com/about-aaoifi/?lang=en

2. Overview of Islamic Financial Instruments in Alignment with Cooperative Values:

• Segregation of Funds: Islamic finance upholds the moral purity of transactions by segregating funds. Funds for Shariah-compatible investments should be separate from those of non-Islamic investments to prevent mixing with prohibited activities.

• Operational Prudence: To maintain compliance, conventional banks offering Islamic products must establish distinct capital funds, accounts, and reporting systems for conventional and Islamic activities.

• Accounting and Auditing Standards: The creation of international accounting standards by the Accounting and Auditing Organization for Islamic Financial Institutions (AAOIFI)[] addresses the need for transparency and consistency in financial reporting across Islamic institutions.

Conclusion:

The synergy between financial cooperative values and Islamic financial principles for financial inclusion is anchored in the adherence to basic principles such as the prohibition of interest, avoidance of uncertain and speculative transactions, and compliance with Shariah law. The appointment of Shariah boards, segregation of funds, and adherence to international accounting standards are essential elements ensuring ethical and transparent financial practices. The alignment of cooperative principles with the key tenets of Islamic finance establishes a framework for financial institutions, including cooperatives, to operate in a manner that fosters inclusivity, social responsibility, and economic development in accordance with Islamic principles.

B. Why Promote Financial Cooperatives (SACCOs) based on the Islamic Financial System?

• Global Growth of Islamic Banking: The majority of Islamic financial institution clients are concentrated in the Gulf states and developed countries, focusing on large business ventures. However, the broader Muslim populations, especially those in poverty and developing nations, have seen limited benefits from the growth of Islamic banking.

• Rapid Expansion of Islamic Banking: Islamic Banking is experiencing significant growth at a rate of 10-15% per year, with over 300 institutions across 51 countries[]. Despite this expansion, there is a notable gap in delivering tangible benefits to the general Muslim population, particularly those in developing regions.

• Underutilization of Islamic Banking for Poverty Alleviation: Although Islamic banking has thrived globally, it has brought little benefit to Muslims living in poverty and has largely overlooked the potential for the development of nations facing economic challenges like Africa.

• Empowering Excluded Muslim Communities: To address the limitations of Islamic banking in reaching economically impoverished Muslim communities, there is a compelling need to promote the organization of Muslim communities under Financial Cooperatives/SACCOs. This model ensures community ownership, decision-making, and equitable distribution of benefits, aligning with Islamic financial principles.

• Permissible (Halal) Financial Services for Sustainable Development: Encouraging the establishment of Financial Cooperatives/SACCOs based on Islamic financial principles is crucial. This approach enables Muslim communities to access permissible (Halal) financial services from their own institutions under their own decision-making in a sustainable way, providing a means to combat poverty through access to finance for businesses.

Conclusion:

In conclusion, the promotion of Financial Cooperatives (SACCOs) by aligning the cooperative principle with the Islamic financial system is of paramount importance. While Islamic banking has shown remarkable global growth, its impact on poverty alleviation in Muslim populations, particularly in developing nations like Africa, has been limited. Empowering Muslim communities through Financial Cooperatives/SACCOs ensures community ownership and access to permissible (Halal) financial services for the broader excluded community, fostering sustainable development and poverty eradication. Governments, NGOs, and development institutions should acknowledge the pivotal role of community-owned Islamic financial cooperatives in improving the social and economic conditions of Muslim communities. Strategic actions, including legal and administrative reviews, are essential to support the growth of these Financial cooperatives as both business and social enterprises, contributing to sustainable development, poverty eradication, and livelihood improvement across various economic sectors in urban and rural areas.

V. Comparative Analysis

Shared Values between Cooperative Principles and Islamic Finance

The shared values between Financial Cooperative (SACCO) principles and Islamic finance practices revolve around their commitment to ethical, inclusive, and community-oriented financial service models. Here are some key shared values:

1. Ethical Conduct:

Both Financial Cooperatives and Islamic finance place a strong emphasis on ethical conduct in financial transactions. They not only prohibit practices such as exploitation but also actively engage in transactions that adhere to the highest moral and ethical standards. Moreover, these models go beyond mere adherence to ethical norms; they are committed to promoting social justice and ensuring the equitable distribution of wealth within the community.

2. Community Focus:

Both models prioritize the well-being of the community. Financial Cooperatives, as community-owned entities, aim to address the financial needs of their members under their member's decision participation, promoting collective economic growth. Islamic finance, guided by Shariah principles, emphasizes social justice and the equitable distribution of wealth, similar to the cooperative principles and values that are articulated about the issue of social justice as a people-centered enterprises.

3. Inclusivity:

Financial Cooperatives and Islamic finance are purposefully structured to foster inclusivity, extending their reach to individuals often overlooked by traditional banking systems. Moreover, these systems empower underserved individuals by positioning them as owner-users and decision-makers, transforming them into investors in their own financial service provider. This commitment ensures that financial services are accessible to a diverse range of the population, specifically including those with excluded financial means.

4. Risk-Sharing and Mutual Assistance:

Both models, Financial Cooperatives, and Islamic finance, are grounded in the principles of risk-sharing and mutual assistance. In Financial Cooperatives, resources are pooled from members to offer financial services, creating a framework where members collectively share in the benefits and risks. Similarly, Islamic finance frequently incorporates profit and loss-sharing arrangements, nurturing a sense of shared responsibility among participants. As owner-users and decision-maker investors, members actively participate in sharing both the profits and losses within the Financial Cooperatives.

5. Democratic Governance:

Financial Cooperatives and Islamic finance institutions commonly adopt democratic governance structures. Members or stakeholders actively participate in decision-making processes as owner-user investors, fostering a participatory approach to managing financial affairs. In financial cooperatives, decisions are democratically made, typically adhering to a "one member, one vote" system, ensuring equal representation and engagement in the decision-making process. When this democratic governance system is effectively implemented, it not only minimizes the risk of fraud within financial cooperatives but also enhances members' sense of ownership, making them true stakeholders in the system.

6. Avoidance of Speculative Practices:

Both Financial Cooperatives and Islamic finance institution models share a commitment to discouraging speculative practices and transactions characterized by excessive uncertainty (gharar). Instead, they advocate for financial activities grounded in real economic endeavors, contributing to the overall stability of the financial system. Financial Cooperatives, in particular, are designed to prevent the financial exploitation often associated with local money lenders, promoting responsible and sustainable financial practices run under the member's control.

7. Concern for Social Responsibility:

Both Financial Cooperatives and Islamic finance institutions place a strong emphasis on social responsibility. They are dedicated to contributing to the well-being of society by supporting community development projects and initiatives aligned with ethical and social values. Financial Cooperatives, on a global scale, play a substantial role in community development projects by establishing cooperative development funds aimed at assisting economically disadvantaged communities. This commitment reflects their dedication to fostering positive social impact and sustainable development.

8. Asset-Backed Financing:

Both models underscore the importance of asset-backed financing over interest-based lending. In Islamic finance, this principle is evident in the utilization of tangible assets or services in transactions, establishing a connection to real economic activities. Similarly, Financial Cooperatives engage in asset-backed financing through capital goods hire purchase or machinery and equipment financial leasing, providing opportunities for economically disadvantaged individuals to participate in genuine economic activities. Recognizing and leveraging these shared values, Financial Cooperatives and Islamic finance institutions can effectively harmonize to create financial solutions that are not only economically viable but also socially responsible. This collaborative effort aims to provide inclusive services for the excluded community, fostering economic empowerment and sustainable financial practice.

Conclusion on Comparative Analysis of Both Financial Practices

In summary, the comparative analysis underscores the remarkable alignment of values between Financial Cooperatives (SACCOs) principles and Islamic finance practices. Both models share a resolute commitment to ethical conduct, community focus, inclusivity, risk-sharing, democratic governance, avoidance of speculative practices, concern for social responsibility, and asset-backed financing.

These shared values lay the groundwork for a harmonious integration between Financial Cooperative principles and Islamic finance law practices. The emphasis on ethical conduct ensures transactions that uphold moral and ethical standards, fostering a fair and just financial environment. The mutual dedication to community well-being is evident, with Financial Cooperatives addressing the financial needs of members and Islamic finance advocating for social justice and equitable wealth distribution.

Inclusivity remains a fundamental value for both models, extending financial services to individuals often marginalized by traditional banking systems. The principles of risk-sharing and mutual assistance are deeply embedded in both, cultivating a sense of shared responsibility among participants. Democratic governance structures give the upper hand to member-owner and user decision-making power, along with the avoidance of speculative practices and a strong commitment to social responsibility, further enhancing the convergence of these two financial systems.

Asset-backed financing, rooted in real economic activities, stands out as a shared value that offers economic participation opportunities, particularly for economically disadvantaged poor community members. Recognizing these shared values, Financial Cooperative principles and Islamic finance law practices can harmonized effectively to create financially viable and socially responsible solutions. This harmonization effort aims to provide inclusive services for the excluded community, promoting economic empowerment and sustainable financial practices. In essence, the convergence of these shared values forms a robust foundation for a more equitable and inclusive financial landscape.

VI. How Practical Financial Cooperatives and Islamic Financial Law be Harmonized?

Harmonizing practical financial cooperatives and Islamic financial law involves recognizing and leveraging shared values, embracing equity-based financing, implementing risk-sharing mechanisms, adopting a community-centric approach, prohibiting exploitative practices, engaging in socially responsible investments, and offering tailored solutions for diverse communities. The synergy between these two systems can create a harmonious and effective framework that promotes financial inclusion while upholding ethical and cooperative principles. Let's look at the detailed breakdown one by one as follows:

1. Shared Ethical Values:

- Financial Cooperatives are based on ethical values such as honesty, openness, social responsibility, and caring for others. They emphasize self-help, self-reliance, and mutual help.
- Islamic Financial Law: Aligns with cooperative values, emphasizing brotherhood, solidarity, and the prohibition of exploitative practices, including exploiting the need through interest (riba) payments.

Synergy: By recognizing and reinforcing shared ethical values, financial cooperatives can integrate Islamic financial law practices to enhance collaboration based on mutual principles, fostering trust and a common ground for financial inclusion initiatives.

2. Equity-Based Financing:

- Financial Cooperatives: Emphasize equity and fairness, with members participating in profit and loss sharing, promoting inclusivity and fairness.

• Islamic Financial Law: Prioritizes equity through profit and loss sharing, ensuring that financial transactions are based on fairness and shared risk.

Synergy: Both systems can leverage equity-based financing models, promoting a more inclusive and equitable financial system that aligns with the principles of both financial cooperatives and Islamic finance.

3. Risk-Sharing Mechanisms:

• Financial Cooperatives: Encourage mutual assistance and solidarity, with members collectively sharing benefits and risks, reducing individual burdens, and promoting community responsibility.
• Islamic Financial Law: Promotes risk-sharing arrangements, where both financial institutions and clients share in the risks and rewards of economic activities.

Synergy: By integrating risk-sharing mechanisms, financial cooperatives can contribute to a more resilient and financial inclusive ecosystem by integrating Islamic financial law, that will reduce vulnerabilities and enhance community well-being.

4. Community-Centric Approach:

• Financial Cooperatives: Focus on addressing community needs, with decisions made democratically by members, ensuring that financial services are tailored to local needs and requirements.
• Islamic Financial Law: Emphasizes brotherhood and solidarity, fostering a sense of community well-being and shared prosperity.

Synergy: A community-centric approach, driven by cooperative principles and Islamic finance law, can result in financial services that are not only responsive to local needs but also promote a sense of shared responsibility and prosperity within the community. Building a sense of shared responsibility within the community ensures sustainable development, as it encourages collective efforts and collaboration towards common goals.

5. Prohibition of Exploitative Practices:

- Financial Cooperatives: Counter exploitation and prioritize member welfare over profit maximization, guided by values such as honesty and social responsibility. For instance, Financial Cooperatives originated in Germany in 1846 during an agricultural crisis and famine to address the fundamental human need for saving and borrowing mechanisms, minimizing risk, and avoiding dependence on local moneylenders.
- Islamic Financial Law: Prohibits interest (riba), preventing exploitative lending practices and promoting fairness and ethical conduct.

Synergy: By jointly upholding the prohibition of exploitative practices, financial cooperatives can create a financial inclusive landscape by using Islamic financial law practices that prioritizes ethical conduct and member welfare.

6. Socially Responsible Investments:

- Financial Cooperatives: Engage in socially responsible investments, reflecting the "Concern for Community" cooperative principle.
- Islamic Financial Law: Allocates a portion of profits for social welfare, contributing to community development.

Synergy: Collaboration in socially responsible investments can lead to a combined impact on community development, aligning with the shared values of financial cooperative principles and Islamic finance laws.

7. Tailored Solutions for Diverse Communities:

• Financial Cooperatives: Financial cooperatives prioritize inclusivity by customizing services to meet the distinct needs of diverse communities. This approach, driven by user-member decisions, fosters financial inclusion at the local level. Services are specifically tailored to address the unique requirements identified by the cooperative members as community members who possess an intimate understanding of their needs in particular and their community in general. This localized approach stands in contrast to services provided by external investors or service providers who look for immediate return on investment.

• Islamic Financial Law: Allows for the customization of products to suit the cultural and economic diversity of communities. The principles of Islamic financial law facilitate the adaptation of financial products to align with the cultural, beliefs and economic diversity of communities. This flexibility allows for the customization of financial solutions, ensuring compatibility with the values and preferences of cooperatives and different communities.

Synergy: By combining efforts to tailor financial solutions, financial cooperatives can integrate Islamic financial law to address the specific economic and cultural contexts of diverse communities, enhancing accessibility and relevance. By synergizing efforts, financial cooperatives can integrate Islamic financial law into their operations, creating tailored solutions that resonate with the specific economic and cultural contexts of diverse communities. This collaborative approach enhances the accessibility and relevance of financial services, promoting a harmonious blend of cooperative principles and Islamic financial law. The combined strength of these approaches contributes to a more inclusive and community-centric financial ecosystem.

In conclusion, the harmonization of practical financial cooperatives and Islamic financial law presents a compelling opportunity to create a financial landscape that seamlessly integrates shared values, ethical principles, and inclusive financial practices. The collaborative efforts outlined in this discussion, encompassing shared ethical values, equity-based financing, risk-sharing mechanisms, a community-centric approach, prohibition of exploitative practices, socially responsible investments, and tailored solutions for diverse communities, showcase the potential for a harmonious coexistence. The comprehensive synergy between financial cooperatives and Islamic financial law not only eliminates conflicts but also fosters a genuine application of cooperative principles, revealing a harmonious coexistence without inherent contradictions. Financial cooperatives/SACCO Societies, through Shariah-compliant financial services, stand poised to serve the financial needs of low and middle-income Muslim communities efficiently and competitively.

Furthermore, supporting the engagement of financial cooperatives/SACCO Societies in shariah-based financing holds the promise of bolstering the real economic sector, contributing to the overall societal well-being of communities at large. This harmonized framework, built on collaboration and mutual principles, not only promotes financial inclusion for the excluded Muslim community but also upholds the ethical and cooperative values essential for sustainable and inclusive societal development. Through these combined efforts, a harmonious and effective financial framework can be established, offering a model for practical financial inclusion that transcends cultural and economic diversities.

VII. Implementing Islamic Financial law in Financial Cooperative Principles

The first step for Implementing Islamic Financial law in Financial Cooperative is establish legal framework to Align the Principles and practices of both models, then create enabling environment to promote Islamic Financial law based Financial Cooperatives by continues grafting and revising training manuals for continues sustainable improvement of financial services.

Implementing Islamic Financial Law in Financial Cooperatives involves a thoughtful integration of key Islamic finance law principles within the existing framework of Financial Cooperatives (SACCOs) principles. In order to establish a logical flow in implementing Islamic Financial Law based Financial Cooperatives, the suggested order are as follows to begin with: -

1. **Educational Initiatives:** Initiate comprehensive training programs for members, elected board members, and professional management staff of Financial Cooperatives, as well as government agencies responsible for cooperative promotion and regulation. These programs should prioritize imparting knowledge about Islamic financial principles and practices, emphasizing areas of alignment with financial cooperative practices. The aim is to ensure a clear understanding of Shariah-compliant practices in the services provided by Financial Cooperatives.

2. **Shariah Advisory Board:** Establish a external Shariah Advisory Board or committee responsible for providing technical support to the elected leadership and professional management of Financial Cooperatives. This board, consisting of religious leaders, Islamic scholars or experts in Islamic finance. This board plays a crucial role in offering guidance on adherence to Shariah principles and ensuring

compliance in all financial activities undertaken by the Financial Cooperative.

3. Strategic Planning: Develop a comprehensive strategic plan that outlines the mission, vision, and goals of the Financial Cooperative based on Islamic Financial practices. Align strategic objectives of Financial Cooperative principles with the Shariah-compliant finance.

4. Identify Financial products to start with: Emphasize the step-by-step introduction and integration of financial products into financial cooperative practices, strategically implementing them instead of introducing a full range of Islamic finance products at once. This step-by-step integration ensures that the external Shariah Advisory Board or committee, elected leadership, and professional management actively engage in the practical implementation of these products. This approach allows for a gradual alignment of financial cooperative practices with Islamic finance principles, providing valuable lessons from day-to-day practices. The involvement of key stakeholders ensures a smooth integration and compliance with Shariah principles in the cooperative's financial offerings.

Note: Of all the products, it is not advisable to start with **Doing Business by Delegation (Wakalah),**Charitable Loan (Qard al-Hasanah) and Gift (Hibah)in a new financial cooperative. Implementing these products requires careful consideration and preparation, especially for a new financial cooperative. In practicing Charitable Loan (Qard al-Hasanah) and Gift (Hibah), the leadership needs to develop skills, and the financial cooperative must build enough social funds from its net surplus accumulation.

5. Professional Management staff: - Professional management is pivotal for the success and sustainability of Financial Cooperatives as financial institutions. Development institutions and NGOs must dedicate efforts to empower leaders and incentivize them to hire skilled professionals. These professionals, including manager, accountants, and marketing experts, are initially brought on board through a cost-sharing arrangement between Development institutions and the Financial Cooperatives, with clear exit arrangements.

Example: In the first year, the cost-sharing ratio may be 75% covered by the Development institution and 25% by the Financial Cooperative. In the second year, a 50-50% sharing ratio should be adopted. By the third year, the ratio shifts to 25% covered by the Development institution and 75% by the Financial Cooperative. Ultimately, in subsequent years, the Financial Cooperative bears 100% of the salaries.

This gradual transition in the cost-sharing arrangement instills confidence. It allows them time to generate more income and strategically plan for self-financing. This approach, as opposed to management solely by the elected board, is seen as essential for the sustained viability and success of Financial Cooperatives.

6. Profit and Loss Sharing: Integrate profit and loss-sharing mechanisms within the cooperative structure. Members should share both profits and losses, promoting a sense of shared responsibility from the outset. Mechanisms need to be designed to help members understand that they are owner-users and ultimate decision-makers in all financial activities and transactions of their financial cooperatives. It is crucial to convey that all other stakeholders, including the external Shariah Advisory Board or committee and professional management, are there to provide technical and legal assistance, enhancing the efficiency and inclusivity of financial services but they are not there to make final decision, as the financial cooperatives owned by members; the final decision makers.

7. Transparent Governance: Enhance transparency in Financial cooperative governance structures, recognizing that good governance and member participation are at the core of cooperative vitality. Ensure that decision-making processes are transparent and inclusive, aligning with democratic governance principles in Financial Cooperatives.

Transparency is crucial for realizing the efficiency and inclusivity of financial services in cooperatives. Without transparency, the cooperative's health and the active involvement of its members cannot be fully achieved whatever we think. When this transparent governance system is effectively implemented, it not only minimizes the risk of fraud within financial cooperatives but also enhances members' sense of ownership, making them true stakeholders in the system.

8. Community Engagement: Community engagement serves as a cornerstone for community-based economic development, with financial cooperatives playing a pivotal role in facilitating this process. Cultivate community awareness by elucidating the integration of Islamic financial principles, underscoring the cooperative's dedication to Shariah compliance and ethical financial practices. Emphasize the significance of involving community members in decision-making processes, both as member-users and member-owners, to ensure the success of community-based economic development. Stress the pivotal role of community engagement in enhancing the efficiency and inclusivity of financial services for community members. Educate the community on the distinctions between financial cooperatives and traditional banking institutions, fostering a deeper understanding of the cooperative's unique principles and contributions to community development. Initiate community engagement practices by involving community and spiritual or religious leaders, as well as influential figures within the community. This engagement with spiritual/religious leaders ensures the dissemination of information through trusted channels and establishes a robust foundation for broader community involvement.

Member-Centric Approach: Positioning the financial well-being of members as the top priority in decision-making processes is integral. Cultivate a culture of financial inclusion that addresses the diverse needs of the community. This strategic approach not only contributes to creating a supportive environment but also reinforces the cooperative's steadfast commitment to ethical financial practices.

9. Review Legal Documentation: Continuously review and revise legal documentation, including Accounting, Corporate Governance, Business Ethics, and Fraud Prevention, to ensure that the governing documents of Financial Cooperatives explicitly incorporate provisions for adherence to Islamic financial principles. This process may involve updating bylaws, policies, and procedures to reflect Shariah-compliant financial activities. Regular reviews are essential not only to maintain alignment with evolving Shariah compliance standards and Financial Cooperative practices but also to ensure legitimacy in Accounting, Corporate Governance, Business Ethics, and Fraud Prevention. This facilitates better engagement with updated financial services and instruments that better respond to members' needs.

10. Product Development: Encourage continuous review and adaptation of existing financial products to align with Islamic financial principles and financial cooperative practices. Motivate collaborative allocation of a research budget among financial cooperatives to conduct a gap analysis of Islamic financial-based Financial Cooperative services. The research aims to develop new permissible financial products that facilitate better engagement with updated financial services and instruments, addressing the evolving needs of members. This collaborative approach ensures the creation of innovative and Shariah-compliant financial solutions that cater to the dynamic requirements of members.

11. Financial Cooperative's Fraud Prevention and Controlling Procedures: Recent fraud reports in Indonesian BMTs (Islamic cooperatives)[14] serve as a crucial lesson to learn from. While these financial cooperatives in Indonesia have shown rapid growth in delivering financial services to the predominantly excluded Muslim community, the occurrence of several frauds in recent years has resulted in significant socio-economic damage to communities. Therefore, as a prerequisite for the promotion of Islamic Financial Service-based financial cooperatives, there must be a well-established set of Fraud Prevention and Control Procedures in place. This practical framework is essential to proactively prevent and mitigate socio-economic damage to communities, ensuring the sustained role of financial cooperatives in realizing financial inclusion.

12. Continuous Improvement: Establish a system for continuous improvement in their Accounting, Corporate Governance & Business Ethics handling. Regularly assess the effectiveness of the Islamic financial services implemented by financial cooperatives, seek feedback from members, non-members, religious leaders, stakeholders, and make continuous assessments and adjustments as needed to enhance alignment of Financial Cooperative practices with Islamic financial law. This ongoing evaluation and improvement process will ensure the sustained effectiveness and relevance of the implemented measures, fostering continuous alignment with Islamic financial principles and meeting the evolving needs of the community, thus promoting inclusive financial services.

13. Partnerships with Islamic Institutions: Explore collaborations with Islamic financial institutions or organizations. These partnerships can provide additional resources, expertise, and support in aligning Islamic financial practices with Financial Cooperatives. Additionally, there is a win-win opportunity for both Islamic financial institutions and Financial Cooperatives, as the latter can become a wholesaling channel for Islamic financial institutions to engage with the broader community at the local level with low operational costs. This collaborative partnership between both financial institutions will bring more efficiency to the financial market.

14. Compliance Audits: Conduct regular audits to ensure ongoing compliance with Islamic financial principles. These audits can be performed internally by elected leaders and professional management under the guidance of the external Shariah Advisory Board or committee to provide an objective assessment. Additionally, engaging external Shariah audit firms can further confirm adherence to Islamic financial principles and practices, ensuring a thorough and unbiased evaluation of the cooperative's compliance. This comprehensive approach guarantees and realizes the efficiency and inclusivity of financial services in cooperatives while ensuring the sustainable financial health of the financial cooperative.

By systematically implementing Islamic financial law in Financial Cooperative Principles, the cooperative can create a financial environment that not only adheres to ethical and Shariah principles but also attracts members seeking Islamic financial solutions. This approach contributes to the broader goals of financial inclusion and social responsibility.

In conclusion, the process of implementing Islamic Financial Law in Financial Cooperative Principles involves a meticulous journey towards aligning with ethical and Shariah principles. The initial step of establishing a legal framework serves as the foundation for harmonizing the principles and practices of both models. Creating an enabling environment, coupled with continuous training and revision of manuals, further supports the promotion of Islamic Financial law-based Financial Cooperatives.

The outlined guide underscores the significance of educational initiatives, emphasizing comprehensive training programs for various stakeholders. The establishment of a Shariah Advisory Board adds an external layer of expertise, supporting the elected leadership and professional management in ensuring strict adherence to Shariah principles.

Legal documentation plays a pivotal role, necessitating a thorough review and revision to explicitly incorporate provisions for compliance with Islamic financial principles. Product development, asset-backed financing, profit and loss sharing, transparent governance, and compliance audits collectively contribute to the integration of Shariah-compliant practices within the cooperative structure.

Community engagement and partnerships with Islamic institutions enhance awareness and provide additional resources, fostering a collaborative environment. The commitment to continuous improvement ensures the sustained alignment of Financial Cooperative Principles with Islamic financial law, creating a financial environment that not only meets ethical standards but also attracts members seeking Shariah-compliant solutions.

In essence, this systematic implementation of Islamic financial law in Financial Cooperative Principles not only upholds ethical values but also contributes to the broader goals of financial inclusion and social responsibility. By embracing these principles, Financial Cooperatives can evolve into institutions that not only meet the financial needs of their members but also actively contribute to creating a just and inclusive financial ecosystem.

VIII. Indonesian Financial Cooperative's Best Practices

Experience of Muslim Communities served by SACCO/financial cooperatives In Indonesia

In Indonesia, the Muslim community has embraced the transformative services offered by the SACCO Society, embodying the financial cooperative values harmonized with the principles of the Islamic financial system. The application of Sharia (Islamic law) in this financial realm carefully encompasses adherence to acceptable transactions, excluding those involving alcohol, pork, or gambling. Crucially, the prohibition of interest (riba), deemed not permissible (Haram), is rigorously upheld, prompting an exploration into the strategies employed by Islamic banks and non-banks to cover their operational costs without relying on interest from borrowers.

The Indonesian experience with Islamic finance unfolds as a compelling narrative, especially through the lens of financial cooperatives. While it is acknowledged that replicating this experience may not be universally effective, the nuances extracted from Indonesia's success offer valuable lessons. Islamic finance, defined as a financial system rooted in Islamic law (Shariah), manifests itself in two distinct institutional forms in Indonesia:

1. Banking Institutions:

Governed by formal banking laws, these institutions operate within the regulated financial sector, primarily serving individuals with substantial investment capacities and involvement in trade. These banks are not targeting the low-income, broader community in the market and focus on clients with higher financial transaction capabilities.

2. Financial Cooperatives:

Positioned as the semi-formal and informal financial sector In Indonesia, financial cooperatives cater to the middle and low-income groups engaged in petty trade, micro, and small enterprises, which are the excluded majority in the market.

Notably, studies indicate that Islamic financial cooperatives in Indonesia, represented by entities like BMT (Baitul Maal wat Tamwil) and BTM (Baitul Tamwil Muhamadiyah), are distinctively separate from the formal financial sector. Operating under the Indonesian Ministry of Cooperatives, they operate without formal regulation from the central bank.

Despite the recent Fraud reports[15] The prevalence of two types of Islamic financial cooperatives, with BMT accounts for approximately 95% of the sector, underscores their substantial impact on nearly 40 million members, constituting the largest Islamic mass. Similarly, (Baitul Maal wat Tamwil) BTM, representing about 5% of cooperatives, serves 25 million members as the second-largest Islamic mass. Initiated by a group of Muslim intellectuals, these financial cooperatives have successfully delivered permissible (halal) financial products to their members, facilitating the management of their businesses. Noteworthy terms inherent in Islamic financial products include joint venture (Musharakah), profit-sharing (Mudharabah), charitable loans (Qard al-Hasanah), and leasing (Ijarah). Each of these financial instruments adheres to Sharia principles, promoting equity, trust, and mutual benefit between financiers and entrepreneurs.

As we delve into the specific financial instruments employed by these cooperatives, such as joint venture (Musharakah), profit-sharing (Mudharabah), charitable loans (Qard al-Hasanah), and others, it becomes evident that these models foster a symbiotic relationship between financial cooperative values and Islamic financial laws. This synergy not only adheres to ethical and Sharia-compliant practices but also strives to foster financial inclusion, laying the groundwork for a sustainable and inclusive economic landscape.

According to different studies the financial cooperatives in Indonesia, particularly those adhering to Islamic financial principles, offer various Sharia-compliant financial products to empower their members and the broader previously excluded community. To mention some of the key Sharia-compliant financial products delivered by these financial cooperatives in Indonesia include:

1. Cost Plus (Murabahah) Financing:

• Description: Murabahah involves the cooperative as financiers purchasing an asset on behalf of a member the entrepreneurs and selling it to the member at a disclosed cost plus an agreed-upon profit margin. The member then repays the total amount in installments.

• Empowerment Aspect: Enables members to acquire assets (e.g., homes, machinery, vehicles) without engaging in interest-based transactions.

2. Joint Ventures (Musharakah):

• Description: Involves a joint venture where members as an entrepreneurs and the cooperative as a financiers contribute capital to jointly own and manage a business. Profits and losses are shared based on pre-agreed ratios.

• Empowerment Aspect: Provides business ownership opportunities to members through diminishing ownership agreement, fostering inclusivity and community development.

3. Leasing (Ijarah) Services:

• Description: Cooperative provides leasing services where members can lease assets (e.g., machinery, equipment) for a specified period, and the cooperative earns leasing rental income.

• Empowerment Aspect: Enables members to access necessary assets for their businesses without resorting to conventional interest-based leasing and at the end of the lease period members have the right to owned the asset.

4. Doing Business by Delegation (Wakalah):

• Description: The cooperative as financiers or the member as an entrepreneur identifies a feasible business opportunity, creating awareness among low-income members or potential entrepreneurial members who lack access to finance. These members are appointed as representatives or agents to conduct specific feasible business transactions on behalf of the cooperative, treating the venture as their own business. The cooperative continues to provide ongoing technical assistance to ensure the success of the representatives. In this arrangement, the representative members, acting as borrowers, pay a service fee, and profits are shared based on a pre-agreed ratio between the representative members and the cooperative.

• Empowerment Aspect: This approach empowers members by allowing them to actively engage in business activities, thereby contributing to financial inclusion and economic empowerment. Members who may have faced barriers to accessing traditional financing are given an opportunity to participate in entrepreneurial ventures. The cooperative's ongoing support and profit-sharing arrangement enhance the economic well-being of the representatives, aligning with the principles of financial inclusion and community development.

5. Charitable Loan (Qard al-Hasanah):

• Description: Interest-free loans extended on a goodwill basis. Borrowers are only required to repay the principal amount, and they may pay extra without promising it.

• Empowerment Aspect: Provides financial support to members in need without interest charges, promoting ethical and interest-free financial assistance.

6. Gift (Hibah):

• Description: Voluntarily and unconditional gift-giving. Represents a transfer of ownership without any obligation for repayment.

• Empowerment Aspect: Facilitates community assistance and support through voluntary contributions, aligning with cooperative values of solidarity and mutual support.

Indonesian Sharia-compliant financial cooperatives valuable lesson

The Sharia-compliant financial products offered by financial cooperatives in Indonesia serve as a valuable model for other countries with a high financially excluded Muslim population. These products aim to empower members, promote economic development, and address the financial needs of the excluded majority. Financial cooperatives worldwide can learn from Indonesia's experience in implementing and integrating permissible Islamic financial principles-based Sharia-compliant financial products through the following key offerings:

1. Joint Venture (Musharakah) and Profit Sharing (Mudharabah)

Both Joint Venture (Musharakah) and Profit Sharing (Mudharabah) are called Diminishing Musharakah and Mudarabah. The Diminishing Musharakah and Mudarabah are two financial concepts commonly used in Islamic finance. Let's explore each of them:

1.1 Diminishing Musharakah:

Diminishing Musharakah is a form of partnership in Islamic finance where two parties enter into a joint venture to own an asset or undertake a business activity. One party, typically a financial institution, provides the majority of the capital as a financier, while the other party as an entrepreneur, often an individual client or business, contributes a smaller portion. The ownership shares are determined based on these contributions.

- Process: Over time, the party that provided the majority of the capital gradually sells its share to the other party or the client. This process continues until the second party becomes the sole owner of the asset or business. The financial institution receives periodic payments, which include both a return on its capital and a portion of the asset's value.
- Key Feature: The key feature of diminishing Musharakah is the gradual reduction of one party's share as a financier, leading to eventual sole ownership by the other party as an entrepreneur.

Note: **Musharakah** is a joint venture, a business partnership where two or more investors contribute capital for investment, profits and losses are shared based on a pre-agreed ratio or according to equity contributions.

1.2 Definition: Mudarabah:

Mudarabahis a form of Islamic partnership where one party provides capital (Rab-ul-Maal) and another party contributes expertise or labor (Mudarib) to undertake a business venture. The profits generated from the venture are shared between the two parties based on a pre-agreed profit-sharing ratio, while losses, if any, are borne solely by the capital provider.

Role of Parties:

- **Rab-ul-Maal**, the investor who provides the capital.
  Mudarib, the entrepreneur or manager who contributes skills and effort.
- **Profit Sharing**: The profit-sharing ratio is determined at the beginning of the venture, and entrepreneur (Mudarib) is entitled to a share of the profits for their efforts. However, in case of losses, the financier (Rab-ul-Maal) bears the entire loss, and the Mudarib does not suffer any financial loss beyond the effort and time invested.
- **Key Feature**: Mudarabah emphasizes the sharing of profits and risks between the capital provider and the entrepreneur.

In summary, **Diminishing Musharakah** involves a gradual reduction of one party's ownership share in a joint venture, leading to eventual sole ownership by the other party. On the other hand, **Mudarabah** is a partnership where one party provides capital, and the other provides skills and effort, with profits and risks shared based on a pre-determined ratio. Both concepts adhere to Islamic principles that prohibit the payment or receipt of interest and emphasize risk-sharing and equitable distribution of profits and losses.

Note: Mudharabah is a Profit Sharing partnership, A partnership characterized by a collaboration between an investor and an entrepreneur. Profit-sharing is based on trust, with one party providing capital (rabb-ul-mal) and the other managing the business (mudarib). Profits are shared according to a pre-agreed ratio, while losses are borne by the finance provider unless caused by the entrepreneur's misconduct.

Integrating both Musharakah and Mudarabah into financial cooperative practices involves a strategic and thoughtful approach. Need clear guide on how to implement these Islamic financial products within the framework of a financial cooperative: By systematically implementing Musharakah and Mudarabah within financial cooperatives, the cooperative can offer Shariah-compliant financial solutions, contributing to financial inclusion and social responsibility. The success lies in thorough education, collaboration, and a commitment to ethical and equitable financial practices (Look the details on **Appendices**).

2. Charitable Loan (Qard al-Hasanah):

Interest-free loans extended on a goodwill basis. Borrowers are only required to repay the principal amount, and they may pay extra without promising it. A modest service charge is permissible for loan disbursement processing.

Charitable Loan (Qard al-Hasanah) can be integrated into financial cooperative practices in several ways, aligning with the cooperative's principles and promoting financial inclusion. Here's how it can relate to financial cooperative practices:

2.1 Community Support and Social Welfare:

Alignment: Financial cooperatives are community-centric institutions with a focus on social welfare. Qard al-Hasanah, being an interest-free loan with a charitable intent, resonates with the cooperative's mission to support the community.

2.2 Member Assistance in Times of Need:

Financial cooperatives aim to serve the financial needs of their members. Qard al-Hasanah can be a tool to provide interest-free loans to members facing financial challenges or emergencies, promoting inclusivity and support.

2.3 Flexible Repayment Options:

Adaptability: Financial cooperatives often prioritize flexibility in financial services. Qard al-Hasanah's feature of voluntary repayment aligns with the cooperative's values, allowing members to repay the loan at their own pace but agreed by the majority.

2.4 Charitable Loan Programs:

Customized Products: Financial cooperatives can introduce specific loan programs modeled after Qard al-Hasanah, offering interest-free loans to members for charitable purposes. This enhances the cooperative's role as a socially responsible financial institution.

2.5 Community Development Projects:

Funding Community Initiatives: Financial cooperatives can use Qard al-Hasanah to fund community development projects. Members contribute to such initiatives voluntarily, and the cooperative provides interest-free loans for projects that benefit the community. Usually this can be sourced from the accumulated social fund of the cooperative.

2.6 Building Trust and Member Engagement:

Strengthening Relationships: Qard al-Hasanah initiatives strengthen the trust and engagement between the financial cooperative and its members. Members appreciate the cooperative's commitment to their well-being.

2.7 Compliance with Ethical Principles:

Adherence to Islamic Finance Principles: If the financial cooperative follows Islamic finance principles, integrating Qard al-Hasanah aligns with the prohibition of interest (riba) and promotes ethical financial practices.

2.8 Educational Initiatives:

Awareness and Understanding: Financial cooperatives can educate members about Qard al-Hasanah and its benefits, fostering awareness of interest-free financial alternatives and promoting financial literacy. By incorporating Charitable Loan (Qard al-Hasanah) into financial cooperative practices, cooperatives can enhance their social impact, meet the financial needs of members responsibly, and contribute to the overall well-being of the community they serve.

Note: this product is not advisable to start with a new financial cooperative. implementing Charitable Loan (Qard al-Hasanah) requires careful consideration and preparation, especially for new financial cooperative. Practicing Charitable Loan (Qard al-Hasanah) the leadership need to develop skill and the financial cooperatives has to build enough social funds from its net surplus accumulation.

In summary, the implementation of Charitable Loan (Qard al-Hasanah) should be a well-planned and gradual process, considering the financial, educational, and regulatory aspects. It's essential to ensure that the cooperative is well-prepared and has the necessary resources and capabilities to manage interest-free loans responsibly.

3. Doing Business by Delegation (Wakalah):

Wakalah is an Islamic financial concept where an individual appoints a representative or agent to conduct business transactions on their behalf. The appointed representative acts as an agent, managing specific business activities, and earning a service fee for their services. A person appoints a representative to conduct business on their behalf. Borrowers pay a service fee, and profits are shared according to a pre-agreed ratio.

By integrating Wakalah into financial cooperative practices, cooperatives can offer a Shariah-compliant Avenue for members to engage in business activities, contributing to financial inclusion and economic empowerment. The emphasis should be on education, transparency, and a commitment to ethical financial practices.

In this Islamic financial concept, the financial cooperative appoints a representative-member or a group of members as agents to conduct specific, feasible business transactions on behalf of the financial cooperative, with a thorough study of business feasibility. The representative can be an individual-member or a group of members chosen based on their skills, expertise, and interest in the business project.

Note: Conceptually, financial cooperatives, as financial institutions, cannot directly engage in business activities beyond financial transactions and intermediation. However, by employing the Wakalah concept, financial cooperatives can identify viable business projects that are then managed by members who act as representatives or agents. The business feasibility might be conducted by interested members and present to the cooperative, or the financial cooperative or community economic development partners or jointly.

This approach enables low-income excluded members to actively participate in economic activities, contributing to financial inclusion and empowerment within the ethical framework of Islamic finance. The cooperative's role is to conduct a thorough business feasibility study, provide training to interested members, offer financial and technical support, ensure compliance with Shariah principles, and share in the outcomes of the business endeavors. Profits generated from these business activities are shared based on a pre-agreed ratio between the financial cooperative and the individual or a group of members (agent) who managed the business.

Remark: Unless the financial cooperative has a team responsible and capable of doing business feasibility study and technical support, it is not advisable to engage in this Wakalah concept-based financial service to start with.

4. Transferring Money (Hawalah):

An agreement where a financial institution to transfer money (receive and send), in return get a service fee. Hawalah is an informal, ancient Islamic money transfer system where funds are transferred from one party to another without the physical movement of currency. This system relies on trust and a network of brokers or intermediaries to facilitate quick and efficient cross-border transactions.

Integration into Financial Cooperative Services: Financial cooperatives can integrate Hawalah as a money transfer service, providing members with a convenient and trust-based method for cross-border transactions. This can be achieved through partnerships with established money transfer networks (Hawaladars) or by establishing an internal network within and among Financial cooperatives for such transfers. The cooperative would ensure compliance with regulatory requirements, transparency in fees, and the security of the transaction process. Integration of Hawalah aligns with the cooperative's commitment to providing diverse, member-centric financial services while adhering to Islamic principles.

5. Gift (Hibah):

Gift (Hibah) is an Islamic financial concept, voluntarily and unconditional gift-giving, often used in the context of financial transactions. In Islamic finance, it represents a transfer of ownership without any obligation for repayment.

Integration into Financial Cooperative Services: Financial cooperatives can integrate Hibah as a product to facilitate member support or community assistance. This can involve creating a fund for voluntary contributions, where members can donate funds for the benefit of others in need and the Financial cooperatives accumulate social funds from its net surplus. The cooperative ensures transparency in fund management, compliance with Islamic principles, and fair distribution of the gifts. Integrating Hibah aligns with the cooperative's commitment to solidarity and community well-being, fostering a sense of mutual support among members. The cooperative would play a facilitating role, ensuring the proper handling and distribution of voluntary gifts within the ethical framework of Islamic finance.

Note: Member's savings and members' share capital can't be allocated for Gift (Hibah). Financial cooperatives should accumulate sufficient social funds from their net surplus before starting such financial services. The initiation of Hibah as a product depends on members' voluntary contributions. unless Members donate funds for the benefit of others in need and the Financial cooperatives accumulate social funds from its net surplus, it is not advisable to start as a service.

6. Safekeeping (Wadiah):

Safekeeping (Wadiah) is an Islamic financial concept where the financial institution acts as a keeper and trustee of funds (refers to safekeeping or custody of funds), where a person deposits their money with the institution(custodian). The custodian is responsible for the safekeeping of the funds. In return, the custodian may pay a gratuitous reward (hibah) to the depositor voluntarily in a form of appreciation. Depositors are guaranteed a refund of the entire or part of the deposit on demand.

Integration into Financial Cooperative Services: Financial cooperatives can integrate Wadiah as a safekeeping product for their members. Members can deposit funds with the cooperative for safe custody, and the cooperative, as the custodian, ensures the security of these funds. While Wadiah typically does not involve the custodian generating profits from the deposited funds, financial cooperatives can offer a voluntary reward (hibah) to depositors as a gesture of appreciation. This aligns with the principles of safekeeping and transparency within the ethical framework of Islamic finance. The cooperative plays a custodial role, providing members with a secure place to deposit their funds without engaging in profit-seeking activities with those deposits.

7. Cost Plus (Murabahah):

Cost Plus (Murabahah) is an Islamic financial concept that involves a cost-plus sale, where a financial institution (seller) discloses the cost of an asset to the buyer and adds an agreed-upon profit margin (sale of goods at a price that includes a pre-agreed profit margin). The buyer then pays the total amount in installments. The financial institution is compensated for the time value of money.

Integration into Financial Cooperative Services: Financial cooperatives can integrate Murabahah as a financing product for their members. This involves the cooperative purchasing an asset on behalf of a member and selling it to the member at a disclosed cost plus an agreed-upon profit margin. The member then repays the total amount in installments. This product allows members to acquire assets such as homes, productive machineries or vehicles without engaging in interest-based transactions. The cooperative plays the role of the seller and financier, ensuring transparency in pricing and adherence to Islamic financial principles. Integrating Murabahah aligns with the cooperative's commitment to providing Shariah-compliant financing options to its members.

Note: It's crucial to emphasize that the asset to be purchased through this financial product (e.g., homes, productive machinery, or vehicles) should be identified by the member-customer based on their interests, not the preferences of the cooperative leadership or staff. This approach aims to prevent post-purchase complaints and ensures that the cooperative's services align with the genuine needs and preferences of its members.

8. Leasing (Ijarah):

Leasing (Ijarah): is defined as financial product where involves selling ofthe benefit of use or service for a fixed price or wage. Leasing (Ijarah) is an Islamic financial concept that involves a lessor (owner) leasing an asset to a lessee (user) for an agreed-upon period and rental amount.

The lessor retains ownership of the asset, while the lessee utilizes it by making regular rental payments. At the end of the lease term, the lessee may have the option to purchase the asset at an agreed-upon price or return it. The financial institution makes assets/equipment available to customers for a fixed period and price by making supply agreement with known equipment suppliers. These financial instruments not only adhere to Islamic principles but also contribute to the financial well-being and inclusive economic development of the community.

In summary, Leasing (Ijarah involves leasing an asset with ownership retained by the lessor, while Cost-Plus (Murabahah) is a cost-plus sale where the buyer becomes the owner of the asset upon purchase. The choice between the two depends on the financial needs and preferences of the members and the nature of the asset involved.

Integration into Financial Cooperative Services: Financial cooperatives can integrate Ijarah as a financing product for their members. This involves the cooperative- the lessor (owner) acquiring an asset and leasing it to a member- the lessee (user) for an agreed-upon rental amount. Members can use the leased asset for various purposes, such as equipment for their businesses. The cooperative retains ownership, and members make regular lease payments. At the end of the lease term, the cooperative may offer members the option to purchase the asset. Integrating Ijarah aligns with the cooperative's commitment to providing Shariah-compliant financing options and supporting members in acquiring necessary assets without resorting to interest-based transactions. The cooperative plays the role of the lessor, ensuring transparency and adherence to Islamic financial principles in the leasing arrangement.

Note: Financial cooperatives seeking to integrate Islamic principles as the lessor (owner) anasset, can adopt a strategic step-by-step approach. It's important to recognize that these cooperatives, as financial institutions, are restricted to engaging in financial transactions and intermediation only. Based on this core idea, financial cooperatives should initially focus on internal capital formation through member-share capital and regular membership savings, maintaining an acceptable equity to debt leverage ratio, typically 25%. Once internal capital formation is realized for six months then can start implementation of permissible financial product services with clear strategy and step by step.

The simplified framework for integrating permissible financial products aligned with Islamic finance principles is a strategic step-by-step approach. Accordingly, the first step should be Begin with a strategic plan that outlines the gradual integration of Islamic principles. Avoid attempting to implement all changes at once. Second, Understand Islamic Finance Principles, this Ensure a thorough understanding of Islamic finance principles to align products accordingly. This includes avoiding interest (riba) and adhering to ethical and Sharia-compliant practices. The third step should be developing financial products that adhere to Islamic principles, such as profit-sharing arrangements and avoiding interest-based transactions. Ensure these products are accessible and beneficial to the target communities. The fourth step need to focus on Education and Communication, educate both elected leaders and members, professional staffs about the newly introduced Islamic financial products is key for the success of the financial cooperatives. Transparent communication is key to fostering trust and understanding among the cooperative's stakeholders. Finally Community Engagement, Community engagement is a fundamental tool for community-based economic development, and financial cooperatives play a crucial role in this process. Foster community engagement and awareness about the integration of Islamic financial principles by educating the broader community about the cooperative's commitment to Shariah compliance and ethical financial practices fundamental for the success of the financial cooperative. Emphasize the importance and value of member-user and member-owner decision-making processes in ensuring community-based economic development. Highlight the significance of community engagement in realizing the efficiency and inclusivity of financial services for community members. Create awareness among the community about the distinctions between financial cooperatives and traditional banking institutions, fostering a deeper understanding of the cooperative's unique principles and contributions to community development. This Community engagement practices must begin with community and spiritual/religious leaders, influential people of the community. This engagement with community spiritual/religious leaders ensures the dissemination of information gather feedback through trusted channels and establishes a solid foundation for broader community involvement and understanding their needs. This two-way communication ensures that financial products meet the specific requirements of the community.

This strategic approach contributes to building a supportive environment and reinforces the cooperative's commitment to ethical financial practices. By following this structured approach, financial cooperatives can successfully integrate permissible financial products based on Islamic principles, contributing to a more inclusive and ethically aligned financial system.

Based on the strategic step-by-step approach, financial cooperatives can start integrating the permissible financial products as follows: as an example.

Joint Venture (Musharakah):

- Financial cooperatives, as financiers, can facilitate joint ventures by forming partnerships with members seeking capital: the entrepreneur for investments.
- Members contribute capital, and profits or losses are shared based on agreed-upon ratios or equity contributions.
- Implement transparent agreements outlining the terms of the joint venture, ensuring fairness and compliance with Islamic principles.

Example 1

Consider a scenario where a member borrower from a financial cooperative is planning for trade, agriculture, and investment in other businesses through a Musharakah-based joint venture.

Example: "Diversified Business Ventures Joint Venture"

1. Identification of Member's Business Plans:

• The member, as an entrepreneur, expresses interest in engaging in trade, agriculture, and other investment opportunities.
• The financial cooperative, as a financier, recognizes the potential and decides to form a Musharakah partnership for diversified business ventures.

2. Capital Contribution for Trade, Agriculture, and Investment:

• Members contribute capital to the joint venture based on their preferences and the specific business ventures planned.
• The financial cooperative also contributes funds to support the members' trade, agriculture, and investment initiatives.

3. Profit and Loss Sharing for Each Business Venture:

• Agreed-upon ratios are established separately for trade, agriculture, and other investment activities.
• If, for example, the member is engaging in trade with 40% of the total capital, they would share 40% of the profits or bear 40% of the losses in the trade venture. Simultaneously, the Financial cooperative, contributing the remaining 60% of the total capital needed for that business, would share 60% of the profits or bear 60% of the losses in the trade venture. This ensures a fair distribution of both gains and losses based on the agreed-upon ratios.

4. Transparent Agreements:

• Detailed and transparent agreements are drafted for each business venture, outlining the terms and conditions.
• Agreements specify the nature of the trade, agriculture, and investment activities, roles and responsibilities, and the profit-sharing ratios for each.

5. Fairness and Compliance:

• The financial cooperative ensures that the terms are fair and comply with Islamic finance principles.
• Compliance includes avoiding interest-based financing, ensuring transparency in transactions, and adhering to Sharia guidelines for each type of business activity.

6. Business Operations:

• The joint venture supports the members in conducting trade, agriculture, and other investment activities.
• Profits are generated through successful trading, agricultural yields, or returns on other business investments.

7. Profit Distribution for Each Venture:

• Profits earned from trade, agriculture, and other business ventures are distributed among the financial cooperative and participating members based on the agreed-upon ratios for each activity.

8. Loss Sharing for Each Venture:

• In case of any losses incurred in a specific business venture, the financial burden is shared among the cooperative and members according to the agreed-upon ratios for that activity.

This Musharakah-based joint venture not only allows the member borrower to explore a diverse range of business opportunities but also enables the financial cooperative to actively participate in and support these ventures while adhering to Islamic finance principles. Moreover, it assists the financial cooperative in minimizing lending risk by diversifying into a variety of member businesses.

Example 2

Consider a practical example of a joint venture (Musharakah) involving a financial cooperative and its members:

Example: "Real Estate Development Joint Venture"

1. Formation of Partnership:

• The financial cooperative identifies members interested in real estate project development, whether for personal housing or business ventures (real estate development for market).
• Members and the financial cooperative form a "Musharakah" partnership to collectively invest in a real estate venture.

2. Capital Contribution:

• Members contribute capital to the joint venture based on their financial capacity and investment preferences.
• The financial cooperative also contributes its funds to the project, aligning with the cooperative's goals and investment strategy.

3. Profit and Loss Sharing:

• Agreed-upon ratios are established for the distribution of profits and losses.

• For example, if a member contributes 30% and the Financial cooperative 70% of the total capital, the member receives 30% of the profits or bears 30% of the losses, while the remaining 70% is attributed to the cooperative.

4. Transparent Agreements:

• Detailed and transparent agreements are drafted, outlining the terms of the joint venture.

• The agreements specify the nature of the real estate project, the roles and responsibilities of each party, and the profit-sharing ratios.

5. Fairness and Compliance:

• The financial cooperative ensures that the terms and conditions are fair and comply with Islamic finance principles.

• Compliance includes avoiding interest-based financing, ensuring transparency in transactions, and adhering to Sharia guidelines related to real estate transactions.

6. Real Estate Development Project:

• The joint venture proceeds with the real estate development project, which could involve construction, renovation, or acquisition of properties.

• Profits are generated through rental income, property sales, or other real estate-related activities.

7. Profit Distribution:

• As the real estate venture generates profits, these are distributed among the financial cooperative and the participating members based on the agreed-upon ratios.

8. Loss Sharing:

• In the event of any losses incurred by the joint venture, the financial burden is shared among the cooperative and members according to their agreed-upon equity contributions.

By engaging in this Musharakah-based joint venture, the financial cooperative and its members collaboratively participate in a real estate project, sharing both the risks and rewards in a manner consistent with Islamic finance principles.

Note: In a Musharakah-based joint venture, the ownership structure is determined by the terms outlined in the contractual agreement. Typically, the ownership arrangement is agreed upon at the beginning of the Musharakah and is outlined in the partnership agreement, with the following two common scenarios: -

1. Shared Ownership:

• The Musharakah agreement may stipulate shared ownership between the financial cooperative and the participating members.
• Ownership percentages may be based on the initial capital contributions or any other agreed-upon criteria.
• At the end of the contractual period, the property is jointly owned by the financial cooperative and the members based on their respective ownership shares.

2. Transfer of Ownership to Members:

• The agreement may specify that, upon completion of the Musharakah period or achievement of specific milestones, ownership of the property transfers entirely to the participating members.
• This could be linked to the repayment of the members' capital contributions or any other conditions outlined in the agreement.
• The financial cooperative may retain a share of the profits generated during the Musharakah period.

The exact ownership arrangement is subject to negotiation and agreement between the parties involved. It is crucial to have transparent and detailed terms in the Musharakah agreement to avoid misunderstandings and ensure a fair and compliant outcome at the end of the contractual period.

In this Musharakah-based joint venture financial cooperative, while the ownership arrangement is subject to negotiation and agreement, it is essential for the financial cooperative leadership to remain focused on the cooperative's overarching mission and the nature of the Musharakah type of financing. This Musharakah follows a gradual reduction of one party's ownership share the financier in a joint venture, leading to eventual sole ownership by the other party the member entrepreneur.

With this primary mission, the financial cooperative should revolve around creating opportunities for excluded members and communities by providing financial services that enable the creation of sustainable wealth and improvement of livelihoods. Managing property should be seen as a means to achieve this mission rather than an end in itself.

Therefore, the financial cooperative should prioritize giving business ownership opportunities to its members using a diminishing Musharakah approach, which is a gradual reduction of financial cooperative's ownership share in a joint venture, leading to eventual sole ownership of the business by the members. This includes ensuring that, at the end of the Musharakah contractual period, members have the opportunity to take ownership of the properties involved in the joint venture. The cooperative's commitment to providing opportunities for members aligns with its core mission and fosters inclusivity and community development.

Furthermore, as part of a broader vision, the financial cooperative can explore ways to open up opportunities to other individuals or communities, extending the positive impact beyond its current membership. This approach not only supports the cooperative's mission but also contributes to the broader goal of inclusive and sustainable economic development within the excluded majority. Transparent and fair agreements, coupled with a steadfast commitment to the cooperative's mission, will guide the cooperative in achieving its objectives while maintaining ethical and community-centered practices.

Example 3

Leasing (Ijarah) in a Financial Cooperative

Leasing (Ijarah): Considering a practical example of leasing (Ijarah) involving a financial cooperative as a financier, the lessor (owner), and its members as entrepreneurs, the lessee (user).

1. Identification of Member's Business Plans:

- A member within the financial cooperative expresses interest in expanding their business activities by acquiring farming equipment, construction machinery, or construction or processing manufacturing machineries, etc.
- The financial cooperative recognizes the need for equipment and proposes a leasing arrangement using the Ijarah concept.

2. Needs Assessment and Selection of Assets:

• The financial cooperative conducts a thorough needs assessment with the member to understand the specific equipment or machinery required for the specific business purposes.

• Based on the assessment, it is determined that the member needs tractors and other machinery.

3. Formation of Ijarah Agreement:

• The financial cooperative and the member enter into an Ijarah agreement for the lease of equipment or machinery.

• Terms, including the lease duration, lease rental payments, and maintenance responsibilities, are clearly outlined in the agreement.

4. Acquisition of Equipment by the Cooperative:

• The financial cooperative allocates funds to purchase the required farming equipment.

• The cooperative becomes the owner (lessor) of the equipment, and the member becomes the lessee (user of the equipment or machinery).

5. Lease Payments:

• The member makes regular lease payments to the financial cooperative throughout the agreed-upon lease period.

• Lease payments cover the cost of the equipment and include a reasonable profit margin for the financial cooperative to cover its operational activities related with this arrangement and ensure expansion of this services to the excluded once.

6. Ownership Transition Option:

• The Ijarah agreement may include an option for the member to purchase the equipment at the end of the lease term.
• If the member chooses to exercise this option, ownership of the equipment transitions from the financial cooperative to the member.

7. Maintenance and Insurance:

• The financial cooperative, as the owner of the equipment during the lease period, is responsible for maintenance and insurance costs.
• The member benefits from the use of well-maintained equipment without bearing additional expenses.

8. Fairness and Compliance:

• The terms of the Ijarah agreement are designed to ensure fairness and compliance with Islamic finance principles.
• The agreement avoids interest-based financing, maintains transparency, and aligns with Sharia guidelines related to leasing.

9. Utilization in Operations: Example in Agricultural or Other Business Activities

• The member utilizes the leased farming equipment for planting, harvesting, and other agricultural activities. Same way the member can utilize the equipment or machinery in manufacturing, construction or processing activities whichever the member engaged on based on pre agreed business activities.
• Increased efficiency and productivity contribute to the members' economic growth.

10. End of Lease Term:

- At the end of the lease term, the member may decide to return the equipment, renew the lease, or exercise the option to purchase the equipment.

Through this Ijarah-based leasing arrangement, the financial cooperative supports the member's entrepreneurial endeavors by providing access to essential capital goods equipment or machinery-based assets. This Sharia-compliant solution allows the member to enhance their agricultural or pre-agreed other business activities operations without resorting to interest-based financing, aligning with the cooperative's commitment to ethical financial practices.

The two most common types of leasing (Ijarah) arrangement forms

The nature of the leasing (Ijarah) arrangement can take different forms, typically falling into the two most common types of lease arrangements: either **Operating Leases** or **Financing Leases**. Clear articulation of the terms in the Formation of Ijarah Agreement is crucial to define the specifics of the lease structure.

Example: Leasing (Ijarah) Agreement with Operating Lease Structure

1. Operating Lease Structure:

- The financial cooperative structures the Ijarah agreement as an operating lease.
- Terms specify that the member will use the equipment or machinery for a specific period without a transfer of ownership.
- Lease payments cover the usage of the equipment, maintenance, and insurance during the lease period.

2. End of Operating Lease:

• At the end of the operating lease term, the member has the option to return the equipment or machinery to the financial cooperative or purchase ifagreewith new term at the end of the lease period.

• The cooperative retains ownership throughout the lease period, and the member benefits from using the equipment or machinery without a long-term commitment.

3. Renewal or Return or purchase:

• The member can choose to renew the lease for an additional period or return the equipment or machinery based on their evolving needs or purchase ifagreewith new term at the end of the lease period.

Example: Leasing (Ijarah) Agreement with Financing Lease Structure

1. Financing Lease Structure:

• The financial cooperative structures the Ijarah agreement as a financing lease.

• Terms specify that the member will use the equipment or machinery with a gradual purchase agreement at the end of the lease term.

2. Ownership Transition Option:

• The Ijarah agreement includes a predetermined option for the member to purchase the equipment or machinery at the end of the financing lease term.

3. Lease Payments as Installments:

- Lease payments made by the member during the term contribute towards the cost of the equipment, which means Lease payments made by the member throughout the lease term serve as contributions toward covering the cost of the equipment or machinery.
- Ownership of the equipment transitions from the financial cooperative to the member, which means the lease agreement follows a diminishing ownership arrangement, where each installment payment gradually reduces the financial cooperative's ownership stake in the equipment or machinery.

4. Flexibility and Ownership Benefits:

- The financing lease structure provides flexibility for the member, allowing them to benefit from the equipment's use during the lease period and eventually become the owner of the equipment or machinery.

By clearly articulating whether the Ijarah agreement follows an operating or financing lease structure, the financial cooperative and its member can tailor the arrangement to suit their preferences and financial goals. This transparency contributes to the ethical and Shariah-compliant nature of the leasing arrangement.

However, it is very important to have detail understandings on the challenges and considerations associated with leasing (Ijarah) financial services for financial cooperatives before jumping into it. Let's highlight and reiterate these points for clarity:

Note: Unless the financial cooperative establishes a separate leasing company dedicated solely to operating leasing services, operational leasing can present significant challenges for the following two fundamental reasons:

1. Mission Alignment:

- The primary core mission of the financial cooperative should center around creating opportunities for excluded members and communities by providing financial services.
- Operational leasing involves managing capital goods, which can potentially divert the cooperative from its essential mission of financial intermediation into managing retuned equipment or machinery storage and maintenance.

2. Complexity and Cost:

- Operational leasing requires the financial cooperative to handle the return and management of equipment or machinery.
- Managing the return of equipment or machinery can be challenging, both operationally and financially, for the cooperative.

Recommendation:

To avoid mission drift and ensure a focused approach on the core mission of financial intermediation for the excluded community as well as making owner of equipment or machinery assets gradually, it is advisable for the financial cooperative to prioritize the Financing Lease Structure.

Rationale:

- Financing Lease Structure provides a more aligned and efficient approach, allowing members to benefit from the use of equipment or machinery with an option for ownership.
- This focus ensures that the cooperative remains dedicated to its primary mission of financial inclusion without being burdened by the complexities associated with operational leasing equipment or machinery management in a store, which demand huge human and space as a resource.

By concentrating on the Financing Lease Structure, the financial cooperative can uphold its commitment to providing Shariah-compliant financial services while efficiently serving the needs of the excluded community.

IX. Challenges and Opportunities

Challenges:

1. Educational Awareness:

• Challenge: Lack of awareness and understanding among key stakeholders (policymakers, government agencies, scholars, religious and community leaders), members and elected leadership regarding the principles of Islamic finance and how they align with financial cooperative practices.

• Mitigation: Implement comprehensive educational programs and trainings on this subject matter to raise awareness among key stakeholders, members, and leaders, and potential members of the entire local community about the harmonization of financial cooperative principles with Islamic financial law.

2. Legal and Regulatory Framework:

• Challenge: Ensuring that legal documentation, bylaws, and policies explicitly incorporate provisions for adherence to Islamic financial principles, which may face challenges within existing regulatory frameworks.

• Mitigation: Collaborate with policymakers, regulatory bodies and development agents, explore legal framework of other experienced counties to establish a supportive legal framework and engage legal experts to navigate and ensure compliance.

3. Capacity Building:

• Challenge: Building the capacity of financial cooperative leadership and members, staff, and government agency responsible to promote and regulate to understand, implement, and manage Islamic financial products effectively by aligning with financial cooperative principles could be challenging.
• Mitigation: Invest in training and development programs to equip leadership, members, staff and government agency with the necessary skills and knowledge for successful integration.

4. Resource Allocation:

• Challenge: Financial cooperatives may face challenges in allocating resources for continuous reviews, legal documentation updates, and capacity building, especially without initial support from the government and development agents. This could potentially impact the financial stability of the cooperative.
• Mitigation: Develop strategic plans that allocate resources efficiently, prioritizing essential functions. Explore partnerships with government and development agents for capacity building support. Establish wholesale linkages with Islamic financial institutions to access loanable funds, promoting financial sustainability. Ensure that the strategic plans are aimed at building self-help and self-financing society, dynamic and adaptable to changing circumstances, fostering resilience in resource allocation.

In conclusion, this comprehensive approach is designed to not only address challenges but also to enhance operational capabilities and sustain the financial health of the cooperative. The goal is to foster the successful integration of Islamic financial law with financial cooperative principles, enabling the cooperative to efficiently utilize all opportunities and channel the benefits towards the empowerment and inclusion of the previously excluded Muslim community. By adopting these strategies, the cooperative can play a pivotal role in creating a more equitable and inclusive financial landscape for its members, contributing to the economic well-being of the community at large.

Opportunities:

1. Growing Muslim Population:

• Opportunity: Capitalize on the growing Muslim population, especially in regions like Africa, its Muslim population projected to grow by nearly 60% in 2030[16]. Offering Islamic financial products that cater to the needs of this demographic creates a substantial market opportunity for Financial Cooperatives adhering to Islamic financial law principles.

• Utilization: customize financial services to meet the specific requirements of the growing excluded Muslim community in Africa. This tailored approach not only addresses specific financial service needs and requirements but also serves as a strategic avenue for promoting financial inclusion within this demographic.

2. Community Engagement:

• Opportunity: Leverage community engagement to create awareness and understanding of Islamic financial principles, fostering a sense of ownership and participation.

• Utilization: Implement outreach programs, workshops, and campaigns to engage with the community and communicate the benefits of harmonizing financial cooperative practices with Islamic finance.

3. Partnerships:

• Opportunity: Explore collaborations with development organizations support financial inclusion, Islamic financial institutions for knowledge sharing, resource access, and establishing a network for more efficient financial services.

• Utilization: Form partnerships that mutually benefit financial cooperatives, Islamic financial institutions, and development organizations supporting financial inclusion. This collaboration aims to expand the reach and impact of Shariah-compliant financial cooperative solutions, fostering a more inclusive and sustainable financial ecosystem.

4. Innovation in Financial Products:

• Opportunity: Innovate financial products and services globally that aim to enhance and accelerate financial inclusion. Align these innovations with Islamic financial principles to meet the diverse needs of members and attract a broader audience.

• Utilization: Encourage continuous product development within the financial cooperative, adapt existing offerings, and introduce new Shariah-compliant financial instruments. This proactive approach ensures the cooperative remains relevant and competitive, contributing to the acceleration of financial inclusion.

5. Regulatory Advocacy:

• Opportunity: Advocate for improvements in regulatory frameworks that support the harmonization of financial cooperative principles with Islamic financial law. Such advocacy can significantly contribute to the acceleration of financial inclusion.

• Utilization: Engage with regulatory authorities, actively contribute to policy discussions, and work collaboratively towards creating an enabling environment for Shariah-compliant financial cooperatives. This proactive engagement is crucial for accelerating financial inclusion and ensuring a supportive regulatory landscape.

By addressing these challenges and capitalizing on opportunities, financial cooperatives can successfully harmonize their principles with Islamic financial law, fostering financial inclusion and community empowerment.

X. Conclusion

In conclusion, the harmonization of Financial Cooperative Principles with Islamic Financial Law emerges as a pivotal stride towards fostering financial inclusion. This collaborative fusion of financial cooperative principles and the ethical framework of Islamic finance unveils opportunities for a more inclusive and community-driven financial ecosystem.

As we navigate the intricacies of financial inclusion, it is imperative for all stakeholders—individual members, elected leaders, local and international development partners, and government agencies to recognize the transformative potential of this harmonization. The shared vision of crafting an ethical and inclusive financial environment necessitates collective efforts and a unified commitment to the foundational principles of financial cooperatives and Islamic finance.

Members and Elected leaders, for individual members, this represents an opportunity to actively engage in financial processes aligned with their values and aspirations. Elected leaders shoulder the responsibility of steering financial cooperatives in directions that resonate with the expectations and needs of their communities.

Local and international development partners play a pivotal role in offering support and resources, facilitating the integration of Islamic financial principles within cooperative structures. Through collaboration, they amplify the impact of financial services, ensuring accessibility while being culturally and ethically resonant.

Government agencies, as architects of financial policies, wield the power to institute frameworks that encourage and facilitate the harmonization process. Their contributions significantly contribute to the realization of broader financial inclusion objectives, particularly for the excluded majority. In sending a clear and articulated message, let it resound that the path to financial inclusion lies in the harmonious marriage of cooperative principles and Islamic financial law. It is a journey towards a financial landscape that not only meets the needs of the present but also paves the way for a sustainable and inclusive future. The call is for unity, understanding, and unwavering dedication to principles that prioritize the welfare and empowerment of communities through ethical financial practices.

Muslim Community Spiritual Leaders: The guidance and endorsement of Muslim community spiritual leaders are indispensable in fostering trust and authenticity in the implementation of Islamic financial principles. Their role as moral compasses within communities reinforces the ethical foundations of financial cooperatives and ensures that financial practices align seamlessly with Islamic values. Their endorsement sends a powerful message to community members, reinforcing the significance of ethical financial practices in the pursuit of a just and inclusive society.

Muslim intellectuals: Intellectuals within the Muslim community bring a wealth of knowledge and insights that can enrich the discourse on harmonizing financial principles. Their expertise can contribute to the development of innovative financial solutions that resonate with the cultural and economic diversity of communities. By engaging Muslim intellectuals in the dialogue, financial cooperatives can tap into a valuable resource that fosters intellectual rigor and ensures the relevance of financial services in a rapidly evolving landscape.

Research and Universities as Centers of Excellence: Research institutions and universities with Cooperative study departments serve as centers of excellence and innovation for Cooperative enterprises. Their involvement is crucial in conducting research that evaluates the impact of harmonizing financial cooperative principles with Islamic financial law. Through rigorous academic inquiry, these institutions can provide evidence-based insights, ensuring that the integration is not only ideologically sound but also practically effective. Furthermore, academic partnerships can facilitate the continuous development of new financial instruments and models that cater to the evolving needs of communities.

In conclusion, the call for financial inclusion echoes beyond the realm of financial cooperatives and Islamic financial principles. It resonates in the hallowed halls of spiritual leadership, the intellectual circles of Muslim scholars, and the corridors of research institutions and universities. The involvement of these esteemed stakeholders amplifies the message of ethical financial practices and inclusivity, turning it into a collective endeavor that spans communities, intellects, and academic pursuits. As we move forward, let this conclusion reverberate as an invitation for a holistic and collaborative approach—one that draws strength from the wisdom of spiritual leaders, the intellect of scholars, and the innovation of academic institutions. Together, we embark on a journey toward a financial landscape that not only includes but truly empowers all.

REFERENCES

1. **Can Islamic Banking Increase Financial Inclusion?, Sami Ben Naceur, Adolfo Barajas, and Alexander Massara, WP/15/31 IMF Working Paper, February 2015**
2. **Islamic finance in Africa: Opportunities and challenges, Debashis Dey & Xuan Jin, September 2018**
3. **Islamic finance industry to witness double-digit growth in 2022-2023,Mohamed Damak, July 2022.**
4. **"Islamic Finance: Principles and Practice" by Hans Visser and A. Bakar**
5. **"Financial Cooperatives and Local Development" by Ana Rosa Abreu and Virgílio Borges Pereira**
6. **"Islamic Banking and Finance: Principles and Practice" by Brian Kettell**
7. **"Islamic Finance and Economic Development: Risk, Regulation, and Corporate Governance" by Amr Mohamed El Tiby Ahmed**
8. **The ethical paradox in Islamic cooperatives: fraud cases in Indonesia's Baitul Maal Wat Tamwil, Dian Kartika Rahajeng, June 2022**
9. **"Cooperative Banking: Innovations and Developments" edited by Gianfranco A. Vento**
10. **"Introduction to Islamic Banking and Finance" by Brian Kettell**
11. **"Financial Inclusion of the Marginalised: Street Vendors in the Urban Economy" by Smita S. Apte**
12. **"Cooperative Financial Institutions: Issues in Governance, Regulation, and Supervision" by Sonja Brajovic Bratanovic**
13. **"Financial Inclusion at the Bottom of the Pyramid" by Prakash Singh**